A Note, A Word, A Brush

Ode To The Arts

Poets Unite Worldwide

Fabrizio Frosini

Poems by

Alexandro Acevedo Johns

Ellias Aghili Dehnavi

Saadat Tahir Ali

Anna Banasiak

Lawrence Beck

Tati Ninaria ~ Tatiana Berdennikova

Tom Billsborough

Judith Blatherwick

Daniel Brick

Réne Curtis

Sheryl Deane

Asavri Dhillon

Karen Edwards

Kemurl Fofanah

Fabrizio Frosini

Alem Hailu G/Kristos

Negar Gorji

Simone Inez Harriman

Birgitta Abimbola Heikka

Afrooz Jafarinoor

Seema Jayaraman

Srijana KC Rayamajhi

Joji Varghese Kuncheria

Kelly Kurt

Eldar Kurtovic

Natchai Leenders

Kenneth Maswabi

Mallika Menon

Barry Middleton

Leloudia Migdali

Istvan Dan Molnar Uriel

Anitah Muwanguzi

Bharati Nayak

Valsa George Nedumthallil

Mohammed Asim Nehal

Dismas Okombo

Rekha Padinjattakathu

Marcondes Pereira

Sarah Louise Persson

Dominic Prempeh

Marianne Larsen Reninger

Kirti Sharma

Pamela Sinicrope

Udaya R. Tennakoon

Tze Min Ition Tsai,

Savita Tyagi

Hans Van Rostenberghe

Mithilesh Kumar Yadav

A Note, A Word, A Brush
Ode To The Arts

Poets Unite Worldwide
Fabrizio Frosini

Copyright © 2017, 2018 Fabrizio Frosini
First Paperback Edition 2018
Independently published by Fabrizio Frosini

Editorial project by Fabrizio Frosini
Anthology of Poetry – Contributors:
Fabrizio Frosini, Pamela Sinicrope, Lawrence Beck, Kelly Kurt, Judith Blatherwick, Daniel Brick, Asavri Dhillon, Anna Banasiak, Natchai Leenders, Alexandro Acevedo Johns, Ellias Aghili Dehnavi, Saadat Tahir Ali, Tatiana Berdennikova, Tom Billsborough, Réne Curtis, Sheryl Deane, Karen Edwards, Kemurl Fofanah, Alem Hailu G/Kristos, Negar Gorji, Simone Inez Harriman, Birgitta Abimbola Heikka, Afrooz Jafarinoor, Seema Jayaraman, Srijana KC Rayamajhi, Joji Varghese Kuncheria, Eldar Kurtovic, Kenneth Maswabi, Mallika Menon, Barry Middleton, Leloudia Migdali, Istvan Dan Molnar Uriel, Anitah Muwanguzi, Bharati Nayak, Valsa George Nedumthallil, Mohammed Asim Nehal, Dismas Okombo, Rekha Padinjattakathu, Marcondes Pereira da Silva de Mesquita, Sarah Louise Persson, Dominic Prempeh, Marianne Larsen Reninger, Kirti Sharma, Udaya R. Tennakoon, Ition Tze Min Tsai, Savita Tyagi, Hans Van Rostenberghe, Mithilesh Kumar Yadav

Cover: image from Pixabay.com, used under Creative Commons CC0

ISBN: 9781980584223

... music heard so deeply
that it isn't heard at all, but you are the music
while the music lasts.

Thomas Stearns Eliot
('The Four Quartets': 'The Dry Salvages', V)

TABLE OF CONTENTS

There is none like thee among the dancers;
None with swift feet.

Ezra Pound, 'Dance Figure'

ACKNOWLEDGEMENTS

Although the title of this poetry collection, "A Note, A Word, A Brush", is mine, the topic (the Arts) comes from an idea submitted by Pamela Sinicrope: a very good idea, indeed.

Forty-eight poets —from many different countries (*)— belonging in the free Association 'Poets Unite Worldwide', have taken part in this compilation. My gratitude to each of them.

Yet, a special thanks and appreciation for the work of my associates: Pamela Sinicrope, Kelly Kurt, Lawrence Beck, Judith Blatherwick — co-editors — and, last but not least, Daniel Brick, who's written the keen and passionate introduction.

A product of the collaborative effort of all the forty-eight poets, this collection represents a further step on the path of Poetry. *Ad maiora!*

(*Fabrizio Frosini*)

(*): *Belgium, Bosnia & Herzegovina, Botswana, Brazil, Canada, Chile, Denmark, Ethiopia, Germany, Ghana, Greece, Hungary, India, Iran, Italy, Kenya, KSA, Malaysia, Nepal, New Zealand, Nigeria, Oman, Pakistan, Poland, Russia, Sierra Leone, South Africa, Sri Lanka, Sweden, Switzerland, Taiwan, The Netherlands, Uganda, UK, USA.*

A song to fall like water on my head,
And over quivering limbs, dream flushed to glow!

Elizabeth Bishop, 'I Am In Need Of Music'

INTRODUCTION

by

Daniel J. Brick

Has it been said often enough that the Arts civilized, and continue to civilize humanity? Such an essential fact can never be affirmed too often, especially if we want to increase knowledge and support of the Arts.

If the Arts are to continue their service to civilization, their value must be repeatedly affirmed, until it sinks deeply within people's consciousness and forms a universal bond between the people and their culture. There is certainly at least one art or artistic component that will touch each individual profoundly. Artists who live intimately with and through their given art certainly know how their very existence is blessed, but we must expand that experience to include those who are not artists but rather the necessary audience. They must realize their role as receivers is as important as that of the makers: their appreciation is the final stage of artistic creativity.

Our title for this anthology of odes to the arts —'*A Brush, A Note, A Word*'— refers to three distinct arts, namely, music, poetry and painting. These three will be representative of the vast array of human creativity. There are three components of artistic creation, each will be illustrated by one art form and a representative artist. Below is an outline of this Introduction:

REPETITION: *The Process of Art > Painting > Sonya May*
WORK: *The Creation of Art > Music > Karlheinz Stockhausen*
JOY: *The Result of Art > Poetry > Robert Bly*

I. Repetition: The Process of Art

Repetition is the essence of the Universe and our lives within it. The great procession of the galaxies, with billions of stars in motion, the patterned movement of planets and moons within a star system, the oblique orbits of meteors and comets —all these celestial objects attest to the cosmic fact of repetition. When we scale down our observation and focus on just the earth, we see multiple patterns of repetition in objects and living things.

Nothing is stationary, as time moves through seasons and space is altered by weather, climate and change. And every day we see animals, large and small, repeating behaviors of yesterday, both individual behavior and species behavior are characterized by instinct, which is the engine of repetition. We humans, of course, are less dependent on instincts, because we have intelligence. Certainly intelligence developed out of instincts, transcending their limitations, giving individual humans more options for their actions and the ability to create individual patterns of behavior for that smallest of unit of life, the individual human being, who through analysis of his/her circumstances can decide upon the best course actions, which are then repeated as the most logical, safest best pattern of life.

In the arts repetition is the path of mastery. John Gielgud is said to have performed the role of Hamlet more than any actor in history. Only his innate modesty and respect for Shakespeare's genius kept him from claiming he had mastered the role. Those who witnessed his stage performances several times readily called him the master. A pianist of the caliber of Glenn Gould achieves greatness by rehearsing 'The Goldberg Variations' over and over, performing them again and again, continually discovering new details for each new performance. And the venerable Robert Frost was still reciting from memory poems he had written just before World War I in the 1960s and still charming audiences who knew them almost as well as he did.

I have a friend, Sonya May, who is a painter and a wonderful one. The first time I visited her studio, she showed me her recent works, works in progress, finished works, and copies of works by painters she admired. I was overwhelmed by the sheer volume and abundant evidence of creativity. And she was soon to embark on a new series of paintings she called 'Disconnections', which explored the way models were being forced in postures and poses that are unnatural. She envisioned many paintings, which would embody the general theme, each presenting an aspect of the whole, creating a series which in music is called "Theme And Variations." Each day in her studio she pursued this project, the days blurring together but the number of paintings with their individual merits mounting. Each painting both clarified some aspect of 'Disconnections' and opened up new possibilities for the next painting. But repetition plays a role in the painter's life which is both routine and symbolic at the same time. I wrote a poem for Sonya which closes with this theme. In the poem she is engaged in self talk about both the repetition and the differences:

It's past
five pm ...
So this is the life
of an artist today:
Day in day out
I put brush to paint,
paint to canvas,

canvas to wall. And
it is enough...

II. Work: The Creation of Art

For over half a century, the indefatigable German Karlheinz Stockhausen (1928-2007) wrote and produced performances of countless works of music, each one unique in form and content, each one carrying performers and listeners in unexpected sound regions, even terra incognito. Like many composers, his earliest compositions were scored for the solo piano; he called them 'Small Musical Spaceships And Time Machines'.

But in the phase of his compositional career, he wrote seven huge operas, each one named after a day of the week, the whole series called 'Licht', that is, "Light". He died before he could complete another ambitious project, a musical work for each hour of the day. And his very last work carried the title 'Paradise'. One of his musicians commented that with that title he had completed his life's work, nothing could come after 'Paradise'.

Stockhausen's music is relentlessly avant-garde: to paraphrase the poet William Stafford, he did not want to write good works but necessary works. To that end, he had to work very hard to create an entirely unique form and content for each new composition. But in his philosophy of composition, music already exists in the Universe, and he receives and transmits it so that people can perceive its sounds and benefit from its vibrations. As a composer, he occupies a prideful place beyond egoism, on a continuum between music's cosmic origins and the listener's apprehension of it. D. H. Lawrence expressed this view of the artist in a poem: "*not I, not I, but the vatic wind that blows through me.*"

But even though the music comes to him as a given, he has to work very hard to realize it, to make it manifest to our hearing. About his remarkable work for two pianos, 'Mantra' (1970), Stockhausen wrote, "*I had no ancillary thoughts or feelings; I knew only that I had to fulfill the Mantra. And it demanded itself, it just started blossoming.*" I recognize in Stockhausen an ideal artist who works so hard but claims so little credit to himself.

In 1968 he wrote one of his seminal works, 'Stimmung', for half a dozen solo voices. The works demands utter concentration from the performers and the audience to release its wonders. But hecklers disrupted a performance at the Holland Festival a few years later. They forced Stockhausen and his singers off the stage, and issued an impromptu and incoherent attack on his music. They argued without much merit that since they could not participate in the performance it must necessarily be authoritarian. They declared the work had no social necessity, since it was too abstract for the workers to comprehend. Later, Stockhausen responded directly to that criticism: "*They don't realize that I might be one of the workers who works the hardest.*"

"*One of the workers*": the greatest recognition of the efforts of artist is to acknowledge what she or he does as work, but not work in the sense of a mind-numbing, body-wrecking drudgery, but work as voluntary, fulfilled with joy, a genuine pursuit of happiness. Those who see idleness as happiness and the Lotus Eaters' Island as Paradise will never appreciate this essential fact of the life of an artist: work is the path of fulfillment and treading it for a whole career of effort is the highest joy imaginable.

III. Joy: The Result of Art

My second Poetry instructor, Deborah Keenan, at a writing institute called 'The Loft', was asked how she felt after writing a poem. She said, "*The gap between my elation at finishing and realizing I have to revise, is getting shorter and shorter.*" There was an audible sigh from some members of our class. Deborah had been emphasizing revision for weeks, and downplayed the emotions that attend a sense of accomplishment. She did more than any of my teachers regarding the actual work involved in being a poet.

But to close this essay, I want to use poets and their poems to address the issue of elation, because, however often we have to postpone closure for the sake of improvement, this emotion is an integral part of the creative experience. To this end, I describe 'joy' as the result of creation, in this instance of a poem.

This joy can arise within the poet as he reflects on the creative experience that has resulted in poems. In 'Winter Privacy Poems At The Shack', Robert Bly expresses this kind of joy:

> *Sitting in this darkness singing,*
> *I can't tell if this joy*
> *Is from the body, or the soul, or a third place.*

Or the joy can be an atmosphere which the poet evokes, especially at the end of the poem, so that it inhabits us when we close the book.

Here is such a closing from Elizabeth Bishop's 'The Moose'. She was taking a bus trip through rural Canada when suddenly the wildness of nature was revealed in a moose:

> *A moose has come out of*
> *the impenetrable wood*
> *and stands there, looms, rather,*
> *in the middle of the road.*

[..]
Taking her time,
she looks the bus over,
grand, otherworldly.
Why, why do we feel
(we all feel) this sweet
sensation of joy?

Or the poet may summon us readers to experience with him or her the joy bursting forth from the poem, even as we read it. Here is an example from the beginning of Christopher Smart's 'Jubilate Agno' from 18th century England:

Rejoice in God, O ye Tongues; give the glory to the Lord,
and the Lamb.
Nations, and languages, and every Creature, in which is the
breath of Life.
Let man and beast appear before him, and magnify his name together.
[from 'Fragment A' (c. 1758-9)]

There is another dimension of 'joy', which was articulated by Friedrich Nietzsche at the end of the fourth part of 'Thus Spoke Zarathustra'. His seer identifies this unique joy as "*deeper still than grief of heart.*" Nietzsche's concept is complex but ultimately clear and coherent. We generally think our joy ends when grief intervenes, because now various degrees of sadness occupy the place that was recently filled with delight. This is no doubt true —up to a point. Nietzsche argues through his seer that beneath the inner realm in which joy and grief confront each other, contend with one cancelling the other, beneath that existence in which the opposites fight to a draw, there is a psychic realm in which another kind of 'joy', one that longs for Eternity, is supreme, with no shadow cast over its delight. If we can overcome the hold of "*grief of heart*", we can descend into that realm of eternal joy.

In 1938, as the world was being relentlessly pulled into another world war and efforts to prevent failed repeatedly, W.B. Yeats wrote 'Lapis Lazuli', in which three Chinese seers who occupy the realm of Eternal Joy, have transcended the grief assailing people.

> *There, on the mountain and the sky,*
> *On all the tragic scene they stare.*
> [..]
> *Their eyes mid many wrinkles, their eyes,*
> *Their ancient, glittering eyes, are gay.*

In another poem, Yeats reminds us such joy is not to be indulged in selfishly. The poet whose mood is heightened by this joy that is reborn from the joy grief destroyed must be promoted:

> *My body of a sudden blazed;*
> *And twenty minutes more or less*
> *It seemed, so great my happiness,*
> *That I was blessed and could bless.*
> ['*Vacillation*', IV; in 'The Winding Stair and Other Poems', 1933]

In 1968, the graphic designer, Saul Bass, won an Academy Award for his documentary film, 'Why Man Creates', and 30-minute film has delighted audiences for the last forty-eight years. It is a witty, entertaining and thoroughly unpretentious piece of creativity, made up of a variety of skits, cartoons, interviews, quotations, parables, montages, et al., but nothing lasts more than a few minutes before something else briefly engages our attention. In his film, Saul Bass doesn't lecture us about creativity or even define it. He fulfills that directive many, many teaching the arts now follow: "*Don't Tell. Show.*" He even leaves open whether his title is a question or a statement, because it's probably both. In a closing montage, he shows us many examples of art works, buildings, books that show examples of creativity, but at the end the camera moves very close to a dilapidated stone wall and focuses on a phrase written in chalk, in lower case: "*i am.*" Just a piece of graffiti. Just one person's assertion of their identity before moving on. An affirmation: "*I was here, here is my mark.*" An assertion: "*I lived a life, I made my mark.*" Creativity is the way an individual being stands in their pride of being: it means, "*I am both myself and representative of all of us.*"

This line of reasoning makes all of the arts equal and equally valuable. That is why poets write their poems but read other poets' poems. Why painters leave the paint to dry on their canvases and visit other painters' studios. Why a musician plays another composer's composition on the piano before displaying their latest composition. And it's why poets, painters and musicians support each others' endeavors in big art festivals or in friendly get-togethers or in an anthologies like this one.

Last I was trying to write a poem about the arts in general. It was getting fatuous, turgid, ridiculous. I was about to give up when I found settled on the floor an impromptu poem that I had ignored. I titled it 'Poetry', because that is my personal art form, my way of affirming —"*i am.*" But it expresses the motive force behind every art form, and the creativity embedded in every human heart. Let me close with this universal statement:

> *There is a voice within each of us*
> *which is everyone's voice, there is*
> *a listening within each of us*
> *which hears the beating of a common*

heart, there is a mind everywhere
that spreads its light over all of us.
And all of these things tell us:
We are One. We are Family.

(Daniel J. Brick, St. Paul, MN)

Unfold your flaming wings and cover out of sight
The nets of day and night.

William Butler Yeats, 'The Poet Pleads With The Elemental Powers'

THE POEMS

Eldar Kurtovic, *'Amidst the Artists'*

Natchai Leenders, *'Operation Jumbo Drop'*

Kenneth Maswabi, *'Poetry'*

Mallika Menon, *'Music'*

Barry Middleton, *'The Artist'*

Leloudia Migdali, *'Poetry'*

Istvan Dan Molnar Uriel, *'The Painter'*

Anitah Muwanguzi, *'The Violinist's Art'*

Bharati Nayak, *'Poetry'*

Valsa George Nedumthallil, *'An Ode to Music'*

Mohammed Asim Nehal, *'Ode to the Music'*

Dismas Okombo, *'All I Want To Be'*

Rekha Padinjattakathu, *'Why Write?'*

Marcondes Pereira, *'Bathed By Calliope's Light'*

Sarah Louise Persson, *'Art Absorbed'*

Dominic Prempeh, *'Soothing Songs Of Old'*

Marianne Larsen Reninger, *'Circumstances of Creation'*

Pamela Sinicrope, *'Musicians Pass the Art of Precise Execution..'*

Kirti Sharma, *'Lines and Tunes'*

Udaya R. Tennakoon, *'Poet a Weaver Bird'*

Tze Min ~Ition Tsai, *'Barbarian Beauties'*

Savita Tyagi, *'An Ode To A Doll Maker'*

Hans Van Rostenberghe, *'Oh Poet, Oh Poetry'*

Mithilesh Kumar Yadav, *'Bharatanatyam'*

Thither, from life and all life's joys and pains,
O even wings of music, bear my soul!

Robert Louis Stevenson, 'Music At The Villa Marina'

THE POEMS

Alexandro Acevedo Johns

Ode to Writing

Reality doesn't exist
without promising words
If Homer had not written the Odyssey
Ulysses would never have returned home

Absent the poetry of Shakespeare
Romeo and Juliet would escape
from the sweet poison of kisses
and they would become an old couple
in a frosty marriage bed

If Cervantes had not laughed
at his own miseries
Don Quixote would have wakened
safe and without ideals
when his sad figure clashed
with the furious windmills

So with words we live

as children that enjoy stories

Changing the real world

We learn to be its spell

In the paradise of gods and demons

with the compassion and hate

from immortal people

In this way we become

Slaves, loving of writing

Ellias Aghili Dehnavi

An Ode to Poetry

O' poetry, hail to thy realm
Of mystery and joy
Thy kingdom forever dwells in the hearts of men
You change the evil to good; Amen

O' poetry, thou art the cure
To the weary nature on earth
Like the Holy Spirit refreshes the men
And changes the evil to good; Amen

Renew us, O' poetry, O' love
The richness in abridgment
You give wings to women and men
Change the copper to gold; Amen.

Saadat Tahir Ali

Boboli Gardens

Fresh fragrance floods Boboli gardens
So the sculptor's plaster when it hardens

Orchestras ring with the cadence of bells
Easter eggs glow in their adorned shells

Exotic dyes flow from cochineal bugs
Trace carmines on ochre Mexican rugs

Intricate carved ivory, inset creature bone
Primal paintings adorn caves set in stone

Such elaborate art on the Alhambra walls
Gilded grandeur of ancient papyri, scrolls

Mammoth Moai busts face the pacific spray
Hushed, they echo what the Nazca lines say

Chopsticks adorn tables in a hundred shapes

A Note, A Word, A Brush

Cotton fiber spun to a million types of drapes

Bamboo craftsmen and their matchless skills
In wineries, mopping brows, near ageless stills

Dainty dancing feet, play gentle reeds
Find their milky way, others in painted beads

Anna Banasiak

Poetry

thoughtfully

slowly I grow up

to myself

I distort time

with words

stopped

in the land of letters

I sway in the rhythm of Your metaphors

I hide in the shadow of Your voice

save me

in the sea of fears

and protect me from the world

The Art Of Poetry

Lawrence Beck

The Peril of Comfort

Satisfaction (had I any) isn't much to write about.

A coolly pleasant August morning, coffee,

Money, home from work to wander, lightly

Obligated, through the house and out into

My unkempt jungle of a yard. The wife

Will nag. I'm used to that. The air will

Warm. My daughter and some friends

Of hers will come to swim. I'll go to meet

The guys from work for beer and wings,

And rude remarks, and those vague pains

Which fuel poems, anomie and isolation,

Being somewhat lost among the artless

And the rows of grain, the slowly shrinking

Image of a woman who refused my love,

Remain too vague to tug at me. I'm on

The cusp of satisfaction, stumped. What

Can I write about?

Author's note:
'The Peril of Comfort' is meant to be humorous. It makes fun of the notion that art must be derived from trauma, that a satisfactory life cannot inspire art. It also rather ridiculously is a poem about not being able to write a poem.

Tati Ninaria ~ T. Berdennikova

The Artist's Brush

The artist's brush is a magic wand
Breathing the spirit of a doting bond
Into the hushed motionless flatness
Of a dismal lifeless canvas

The artist's brush has a mind of its own
Gamely curves the line, twirls and goes on
Hard to control, obstinate and bold
It splatters the fountain of gold.

The artist's brush ripples away with laughter
Reluctant to scribble the name of the drafter
And leaps to the centre of the playground
Anticipating another solo round

Tom Billsborough

Commedia Dell'Arte

Leonardo's lines and Titian's colours

Sing out as arias from an opera,

Or a pirouette of the great Pavlova,

Taking your heart into those realms unseen,

Into the reality of dreams.

The Saint John's Passion soars aloft and so

Becomes vast arches for the Cathedral of Rheims.

In Art the structure matters, rhymes like counterpointed

Feelings giving substance to our being.

And ancient myths a new expression,

Or celebrate the joy of living,

Or the tragedy of human errors

In Sophocles and in King Lear

They paint the road to ruin.

Which medium we use is interwoven

With strands of other Arts we know

We cannot stop the inter-flow

Of memories and of our learning.

Our path is colored by our aptitude,

Only varied by the outer form permitted by its latitude.

Verse is what I choose and yet I celebrate

All other Arts and chiefly that of Nature

Whose sounds and sights and scents give pure

Ideas and dreams to contemplate.

Judith Blatherwick

A Poem is Born

The words the poet wrote unfolded
From his prized and blessed pen.
Spilling forth onto blank pages
Lines of swirling ink, and then

Enchantment cast them into letters.
Giving order, meaning, tense
To verses new, borne here from somewhere.
Still the poet knows not whence.

A story to be told starts speaking
In this new poetic realm.
Lines of words sail on the paper,
With the poet at the helm.

The magic threads of ink now woven,
From the book the page is torn.
Read and absorbed by just one reader.
Now at last the poem is born.

Daniel J. Brick

The Muse: Her Presence

This morning, in the gray light

of early winter, I was promised

a poem. "It's waiting for you,"

she said softly. "Look for it

in familiar places near home.

Not that distant home of your origins,

but the one close by, that has served

you so well, in these years of endeavor."

And she had departed, in the middle of

a thought. It's almost a routine by now:

she is summoned by another poet, perhaps

like myself, perhaps not. I don't know –

How many poets does she attend? How does

she determine her visitations? Does she

check names – This is useless and unworthy.

I'm acting like a cast-off lover, a jealous

one, a hurt one... I will soon fulfill

this morning's promise: the poem, already

half written, lies face-down on the table.

What else is there to consider. Oh, yes,

it is the lingering scent of her presence.

Réne Curtis

Brushstrokes

The painter always
Has a plan... it's born
From the mind and
Ends by his hand

Van Gogh closed his eyes
and opened ours
To a canvas of
The Starry Night skies

Monet painted a tune
in his head for us
Waterlilies they danced
To the art of the brush

Picasso 's passion
Les Demoiselles d'Avignon
The beauty of the female
Nude captured and so on

Oh the painter has
Always had a plan
To reveal beauty by
The art of his hand

Sheryl Deane

Knock the Silence

The open book is a journey through time
It pages of history captured first hand
The soulful writer or the artist's brush stroke
Emerge on canvas, bold as fire
Lighting the darkness forging ahead
Bringing silent paths of history to life
Seen through eyes of
The Common Man

The great Masters of Music resound like a gong
Announcing the arrival of new ideas
Tuned to an underlying life force –the silent score
Come to life in a circle of truth
Conducted into our consciousness
Forging ahead with sweetest melody

Gone is the Politicians convincing rant!
Gone is the military dictator's pompous promise!
Gone is the deceit of religious interpretation!

Its pale Image, now twisted by artistic integrity
Which thaws the lifeless page to resurrection
Its life form fills the emptiest space
An encrypted message of truth
Free to all who knock and enter
A mirror of endless wisdom

The Arts —keeper of time

Asavri Dhillon

Expressing is Art

"Beauty is in the eye of the beholder."

Each of four brothers was provided

a blank canvas.

The first one closed his eyes and painted

with his hands,

feeling every move on the rough canvas

as his soul danced.

The second one had a heavy heart,

his soul deeply connected to memories.

He couldn't put his thoughts into figures.

So, he penned down every one

breathing in his conscious, sub-conscious, unconscious mind.

The third one had a soul which converted

every emotion into melodies.

So, he wrote every musical note he could.

The fourth one knew only one way to express himself,

and that was- dance.

So, he danced while focusing at the blank canvas

where the flashbacks of memories and emotions played.

Art provided the lost with an aim,

the broken with a remedy

and the happy with joy.

Karen Edwards

Without Words

The strumming guitar sings of life,
and of cheer, of beauty and hope,
things a heart holds so dear.
Great poets endeavor to instill
such a scene on the stage of
the mind, to summon the feelings
with grand words, verse and
rhyme, to reach that inner ear
of the soul, that takes it all in,
takes over control. The fount
of emotion buried within,
the source of the smiles,
and trigger of tears. The
place where humanity truly
begins. Though music and
lyrics are meant to go hand
in hand, rare melodies written
must alone make a stand,
for the touching of spirit,

the poetry there is in the
language of notes, a combination
of sounds, and the message
is heard quite loud and clear
without a single preposition,
adverb or noun.

Kemurl Fofanah

Benediction from the Art

Have you seen how the artists capture our souls in their minds
How they paste them on the canvases of different reminiscence?
Have you felt how they cause our imaginations to sing,

A thousand voiceless melodies of benedictory song,
Praising each raw line from the waves of stilled motions?
Have you seen the live benedictions gushing from their art?

To the masters of words, the poets, the novelists, the writers,
The melancholic tuners who often call out to our thoughts
From those shallow wandering spaces of joy and isolation

We have heard your whispers, their bittersweet loudness
How they heal wounds, bear love, bridge gaps, vanish races
Letting the whole world bask in the benedictions from the art.

Fabrizio Frosini

Realizing

«*What is Poetry?*»

Heavens no! Don't ask me;

I don't know the answer.

«*Try one —Any answer;*

Just to give me a clue»

Maybe

Poetry is just a starry night looking down at us..

Or it is the whole of

The underground rivers of our daily tears and moans,

Of happiness and grief, sadness and gratitude..

It is, maybe, the sight of

An emaciated body got lost in dusty fields..

A dazzling, unaware smile of a newborn baby..

A sound (*Ocean's voice?*) from the very heart of a seashell..

An old soul in its (*Her/His*) final anguish..

A lover's secret silence lit by the fading light of sunset..

A ripple in the brackish fluid of Consciousness..

Anyway: an endless moment in anyone's life,

Maybe.

«Moments of Life. Is Life the clue?»

It might, if only I knew what Life is.

What I've realized, intertwining poetry and life, is that

We have to add Darkness when we try to appreciate what

Life is.

Darkness.. —A bit, at least. At its heart.

Fabrizio Frosini

('Realizing', Italian version)

Rendersi conto

«*Che cos'è la Poesia?*»

No, per carità! Non chiederlo a me;

Non conosco la risposta.

«*Prova a darmene una —Una qualsiasi;*

Tanto per formarmene un'idea»

Forse,

La Poesia è semplicemente una notte stellata che dall'alto ci guarda..

O l'insieme dei

Fiumi sotterranei delle nostre lacrime, dei nostri quotidiani lamenti,

Di gioia e dolore, di amarezza e gratitudine..

O, forse, è la vista di

Un corpo emaciato sperduto fra campi polverosi..

Il sorriso smagliante, inconsapevole, di un neonato..

Il suono (*Voce dell'Oceano?*) dal cuore profondo di conchiglia..

Una vecchia anima nella sua (*di Lei / di Lui*) angoscia terminale..

Il silenzio intimo d'amante, illuminato dalla luce morente del tramonto..

Un'increspatura nel fluido salmastro della Coscienza..

In ogni caso: un momento infinito nella vita di chiunque,

Forse.

«Momenti di vita. È dunque questa la chiave?»

Potrebbe, se solo sapessi cosa è la Vita.

Ciò di cui mi rendo conto, in questo intreccio Poesia–Vita, è che

Occorre aggiungere Oscurità quando proviamo a descrivere la

Vita.

Tenebra.. —Almeno un po'. Al suo cuore.

Alem Hailu G/Kristos

The Soundtrack Of Life

Yes indeed
'Music is life's
Soundtrack!'
As on the rail of time
An old song verse
Transports us back
A decade or a score
Even more,
To recollect
A quality time
With a lover
We spent
Though probably
Now the boat
Is irretrievably lost.

Or it makes us remember
How with a life partner
We vowed to stick together.

Maybe it mirrors
The grief
When time with our other
Turned brief.

What is more
The things we did marvel
When on a travel.

Also it could conjure up
In our head
A historic water-shade
To a new trend
That allowed a go-ahead.

Negar Gorji

The Painter

Sitting in front of an easel

like she's gonna hug it

Staring long hours at a picture

That nobody can see,

And drawing boundless lines

That come from her heart

and only her paintbrush can understand them

Two hours pass,

Still, she keeps painting,

As she's an inseparable part of it,

Diminishing as the paintbrush does

And will die on that woody chair.

Nobody knows,

Nobody hears her.

While painting,

She talks to that portrait,

And sometimes wells up with tears,

But nobody sees them

The portrait is calm and patient in listening,

He never blames her and is always there to talk,

He never leaves her alone.

Simone Inez Harriman

Ode to the Victorious Youth

Oh ancient youth crowned in glory

Bronzed and symbolic of victory

You were looted, and lost in the Adriatic sea

And drawn from the depths of antiquity

Nameless and naked in the city of lost souls

Your mysteries deepened and unresolved

Your swift feet are gone, you are alone

Torn from your privileged plinth of stone

Detached, unstoppable, determined your gaze

Dedication, discipline, the old ways repay

Silently you speak to all young men

Despite all adversity, you can rise and rise again.

Editor's note:
The term "Victorious Youth" refers to an ancient Greek 'bronze' that was found out in the Adriatic Sea, Italy. It was probably part of a shipment of Greek art artifacts looted by the Romans, when the ship sank. It is currently part of Getty Museum collection, but Italy disputed Getty's propriety, since it was illegally sold to the museum.

32

Birgitta Abimbola Heikka

Ode to the Seer

A story teller, you art
narrating tales on papyrus
of pharaohs and queens

A painter, you art
painting on stones
of animals now extinct

A singer, you art
singing in praise
of times and rulers in transit

A mirror, you art
magnifying man's soul
on canvas, paper and magnet

Sour is the story, at times;
contrary, the painting
and sorrowful, the song

The paper is burnt

The canvas, smeared

The magnet, scratched

Destroyed, you art

and destroyed is man's soul.

Afrooz Jafarinoor

Come, Oh Poetry

Oh poetry

Come and take me

Take me to your lands

That are as vast as a galaxy,

As tiny as a tear,

As radiant as a flower,

As silent as air,

As passionate as a melody!

Oh poetry

Come and take me!

Without you, poetry,

I am hollow, hollow!

Without you, poetry,

I am not me!

Seema Jayaraman

Modern Art

I strive to be a modern art

As convoluted as I can be

Fitting the meanings of my bane

In the impressionist colors

Trapped in undefinable shapes

I find myself spiraling

To fill this emptiness with verve

Making huge arcs around you seeking

To swing the perfect golden ratio

That kneels to Fibonacci formula

I walk around with blinkers

Lest I be blinded with

the shades of Scarlet

That have overridden

my canvas once douched with

Dashes of ochre, lilac, mauve and pink

I have tried so hard to fit

The points of your triangular views

Into the circle of my embrace

And then scrambled around some

To fill the voids in the arcs

With some verses that no longer rhyme

With no space on the canvas

to rejoice the fine grace of my wrists

Held in 'mudra' in your praise

Author's note :
'mudra' is a hand posture used in traditional Indian dances.

Srijana KC Rayamajhi

White Canvas

I stretch out a plain white canvas
filbert, flat, fan, pointed bristles queue
prepared to paint my unseen beau

outline with bluish loyalty and trust
pinkish tender loving care is a must
brownish comfort, warmth and hope
bright smile, orange joy, lively lope
golden touch, wise line, a muse of mine
then I sprinkle silvery sensitive shine
magenta spirit, greenish growth and vision
I add every stroke of my dreamy vermilion
detail it with passionate red, turquoise clarity
careful to avoid black and gray disparity

Folded arms, I stare at my make
no color seems though to slake
The missing Something.

A Note, A Word, A Brush

I take out my roller brush

recoat the canvas pure white.

Irked I close my purple eyes, breathe out, stand quiet

there I see an ethereal portrait of my real star

Let me embrace you darling the way you are.

Joji Varghese Kuncheria

Margamkali Dance

Far from the Middle East,
No one knows precisely when,
Came this art form to India.
Either the traders of Judea
Or the Jewish exiles in 68 AD
Brought this art form to Cochin.

Through the silk route it came.
Since then it remained with
The people of the New Way
In the southern tip of India.
So integral to their culture,
Has this art form become.

A dozen dancers sing and dance
Around a lighted wick lamp.
An allegorical enactment is this,
With the lamp representing Christ
And the performers his disciples.

'Margam Kali' is this unique art.

"Margam" means path or way,
Traced back from the diaspora
And derived from the Brahmins.
So synonymously is it linked
With the people who are called,
St. Thomas Nasranis of Kerala.

Kelly Kurt

Artistic Sacrifice

The creative person is a masochist

How easy it would be to amble through life

A straight line laid out to follow

Convention and conformity

But the poet and the artist self-impose pain

Dissecting their brains with fiery blades

Pouring blood thick essence into existence

Willing to suffer agony and anguish

Struggling to emancipate muses

To elevate sleepwalkers

Eldar Kurtovic

Amidst the Artists

We dance with a rhythm

Paint with a brush

Write verse with a quill

But it's still not enough

We sway to a melody

Recite poems when it's hushed

Read in the dark

But it's still not enough

We groove with the jazzy flow

Find heartsease in stanzas

Burn portraits onto bark

Even roam to lonely verandas

But all of this is still not enough!

For art is born as unfinished

A product of our daft vision!

A remedy to every souls

Existentialism

Natchai Leenders

Operation Jumbo Drop

Woo or boo to what music you choose.
Do you look up to the 'Boss' Bruce
or to the Liszt of lullabies sung in the Louv-
re with sopranos in a soothing groove,
amusing to the muses and all that jazz?

All that jazz, a mass or other classical masterclasses has more pizzazz
than passin' sassy lasses, spinnin' fast
like 45 RPM records or twirlin' Tazz-
manian devils on Ladybaby's looney tunes.

Looney tunes and daffy dudes two-step soon
on dubstep with tuba, flugelhorn, and bassoon.
Even to the blues, doom metal and MF Doom.
Nirvana of groove to Fighter of Foo and gloom.
Lil' Johns crunk, sex pistol punk. Yeah! I can tell.

Tell, boom-dap, two claps, crews'll dwell

as two lads do dabs to Lose Yourself

and loops have to sap through the shelves

and you sad, who has a noose to hell.

Why are the choirs of heaven hesitant?

Hesitant to tell ya men 'bout sad and sorry sentiments?

But the band, beats, and bars are being benevolent.

Flutes and lutes mute screamin' demons and irrelevant revenants.

Heavy news drops easier like bass parachute equipped elephants.

Yo Dre, operation successful: dropped the ode to the sound of music.

Kenneth Maswabi

Poetry

I don't know your origin, race or tribe

I don't know your extent within the universe and beyond

I don't understand your powerful message at times

I don't know your destiny

I don't know the source of your consciousness

I know that you're a beautiful existence

I know that you're inspiring and full of meaning

I know that you're the best part of humanity

I know that you're an everlasting source of wisdom

I know that you fulfill my wildest desires

I also know that you're ugly

I also know that you're painful

I also know that you're sour

I also know that you're dark

I also know that you're whatever you choose

I've embraced you wholly

I've listened to your words
I've enjoyed your company
I've been overtaken by your passion
I've lost all my questions

I live under the canopy of your words
I sleep under the blanket of your dreams
I have travelled on the path of your imagination
I am blessed by your eternal wisdom

Mallika Menon

Music

Any sound can be music
as there is no voice, only sound, and
even silence has its own cadence.
Tempo, timbre, texture, rhythm
term the color of musical sound.
Music seems as mighty as sea
with no specific end or start.
At times it is like vast azure sky
whose magnitude is ineffable.
In pitch and harmony, superbly,
it can swing up and down.
As music gives wings to the souls,
if we are lost in music, then we
can be lost in an ecstatic world
of endless, euphoric, wondrous feeling
which can land us in Elysium.
When lilt of lullaby reaches ears,
woes melt like fog in sun and it
lulls the mind to slumber fast.

Rhythm of sea tides echo music.
Birdie's chirping turn as chorale,
Humming rain and whistling wind,
very well orchestrated melodies.
When nature opens doors of music
I wish to vanish in its soothing lee.

Barry Middleton

The Artist

the soul of the artist is a burden
we take responsibility for tomorrow
the audacity of the task
boggles the mind

with chisel or brush or pen
we reduce mountains to monuments
we conjure the fire of a starry night
we freeze the scream of terror

and we must chronicle love and death
the beauty of the universe
the grief of letting go
oh this is a heavy weight we bear

art aims to change the world
this is its sacred mission
and some will be remembered
and some will die unknown

and yet when we unite

it eases our burden

to know so many others rise to the call

to fracture the walls that separate us.

Leloudia Migdali

Poetry

Like a magic spell it takes you afar
Beyond infinite insight horizons
Or arcane depths beneath the earth
It mercilessly besieges your mind
Questioning, demanding, begging to get inside,
Luring you to unexplored labyrinths of
Words, words, words, words
Written, erased, rewritten, deleted
Till they transform into firing arrows,
A shot of elixir for a quenching heart.
Notes, smudges, crumbled papers scattered around,
In the house, at the café by the river
Under the orange tree in the yard.
Sweet surrender when mind yields
Butterflies and demons together
As heartfelt thoughts
Become a poetic string.

Istvan Dan Uriel Molnar

The Painter

silence has no words

the picture of life, glimpses

of lifeless bodies forever

while sea storms motionless

not a drop of souls

flows outside frames

poet looks for elements

in the ocean as roaring

flow and staring eyes cry

in distress and seek

their fate in enigmatic heaven

the faces perceive

how the vulnerable body

soul and spirit escape

from the humid torque

and the waves are still

in freedom-how the hearts

of life remain secret

Anitah Muwanguzi

The Violinist's Art

Strolling by a sapphire river,

I watched the leaves fall tenderly in hues yellow, lime, and red—

Teased by a gale they danced about my ankles in circular motion.

But oblivious to their graceful display, I pumped my fists at fate's cruel

hand,

kicked the sand on the beach and screamed at the birds to leave me in

peace.

Time and time again I chased love, certain each time would be the last.

I saw him then, seated on the top-most branch of a tree,

drawing a bow across its strings,

then plucking the strings with his fingers, eyes closed;

my skin tingled, and the late afternoon chill seeped into my bones

even as my tongue tasted salt. He played such sad music.

The burnished brilliance of the wood brought thoughts of brown skin

to mind.

Closing my eyes, I let my mind wander

and saw the neck as mine, my upper bout under his mastery.

His finger trail lighted a furnace below the waist across my bridge,

to the fine tuners and tailpiece,

The Birds had quieted, gathered about me in the sand,

each of us entranced by the wailing violinist

whose stroke had gouged my heart free of its bulwarks.

The sun retreated behind the cloud's skirts,

his mind thrown by the pain dripping from his soul.

Thunder shattered the lull and lightning marked the sky

as I remained entranced by the Violinist's magic;

and when rain fell, I was cleansed

even though he never saw me.

Bharati Nayak

Poetry

It is that pain
which torments you always—
it is that sorrow
which wants to come out,
but alas, cannot.

It is that pain
which shivers your lips
and sits as a tear drop
in the corner of your eyes—
it is that ache,
which like an arrow,
pierces your heart.

It is that pain
which sometimes
flows in torrents
like a river
and spreads through

the whole world

like water vapor,

then blooms to beauty

like a flower.

It is poetry

of life—

it is

the rhythmic dance

of sorrow and happiness

woven into words.

Valsa George Nedumthallil

An Ode to Music

Music, Oh mysterious sprite!
Lift us to the seamless realms of delight
Your ubiquitous presence we feel;
In the hum of crickets, in the silence of the stars
In the falling cataracts, in the running streams
You are there in the lone sea breakers
And under the swift wings of the wind

Come as subtle vibes to saturate our being,
Winding your way through every sinew
Enfold us in your rapturous hold,
Raising our souls to the magic of rhapsody
Paint intangible pictures in silence,
Creating a sensation beyond the reach of words
Let our souls savor the taste of ecstasy,
Daubing myriad hues on all ugly stains
Land us in the sequestered pools of oases,
As the blistering sands leave burns on our souls

Oh Music! Come and fill me

Soak me from foot to crown like a falling drizzle

Like a caressing soft wind

Like a marauding sensation

Drown me in the subaqueous quietude of the sea

Levitating me through ether

And lifting me up onto the borders of heaven!

Mohammed Asim Nehal

Ode to the Music

Lift me up to the sky by the notes
Oh, flute by your captivating melodious tunes

Sing to my body and sing to my soul...

A lifeless journey is becoming meaningless
Let ears be the witness that it heard flawless
Beat your drums very hard on the sadness
And let this mind shed all its madness

Let the salty tears flow in rhythm
Let the eyes shed their entire burden
Let the neck move sideways at random
Make different pitches by using trombone

I don't care whether you're near or far

So long as I hear a song on guitar
Our childhood days I always remember

Running after butterflies or playing synthesizer

Sing to my body and sing to my soul...

When life plays with me Odle-ya-ee-oo
My mind demands to hear Didge-rid-oo
Oh the cuckoos, O Nightingale come to my concert
We shall play tonight violin and trumpet

Look at the sky and see those stars
They are strangers and they are far
In the restless nights they play for me on sitar
I sing with them by playing my guitar

Sing to my body and sing to my soul...

Dismas Okombo

All I Want To Be

All I want to be is a writer,
to write throughout the winter
about the beauty of summer's sun,
to pen the lonesome moon
and the twinkling stars,
to scribble the serenity at noon,
sometimes describing the ranging sea
yet other times explaining the buzzing bees.
It's awesome to be a writer
and enjoy the beauty of nature.

Writers maintain their inner peace
they're never worried over their pace,
their steps are measured.
Their movements are purposeful.
They send profound messages,
in their moments of silence.

Always their hearts are

o'er flowing with tender love,
Always their faces are
radiating a genuine smile,
Always their eyes are
warmly welcoming.

At the end of their story
there is a reason to believe
At the end of their journey
you find a reason to live.

Rekha Padinjattakathu

Why Write?

Why do you write poems, they ask;
Why waste your time?

Learn; Go to work and earn
Or just be home;
Play with the kids, rave about their skills
Keep the house spick and span
Maybe whip up a dish to gorge;
Why waste your time writing,
When you could just let it be!

What do they know
Of the travails of a feeling heart,
That wouldn't stop aching for days,
For a dead sparrow by the street;
That wouldn't stop bleeding,
For a child in pain across the seas;
That has forever, clinkers burning in it,
For all that is not fair with this world!

Writing is not for others

Not to seek approval or appreciation

Not for the fame and glory;

It is for me, myself,

To soothe a soul ablaze

To keep me sane, in a world gone insane!

Marcondes Pereira

Bathed By Calliope's Light

I.

Calliope bring to me a golden rhyme,

'Cos I will praise with joy and love.

Some epics which came from heaven above,

II.

Golden was the unreal time

When I read Odysseus epic adventure

Poetry touched me like never before

III.

I dreamed of Vasco da Gama's unreal story

Sailor who founded India, and arrived to paradise.

Loved by nymphs, he deserved a calm demise.

IV.

Won a violent shipwreck, owner of wisdom

He guided Indians towards the light.

Discovery of Bahia`s poetry fills the night.

V.

Calliope is the most beautiful creature

Due to you, I`ve painted a cosmic memory

I lay on my knees and praise you, I've got real freedom

Sarah Louise Persson

Art Absorbed

Art is not a simple thing
But yes it is unique,
Be that art in picture frame
Or a poem that we speak.

Be it that one special song,
The elegant ballet dance,
A stage play scene of tragic form,
Or a photo we enhance.

The music paints a picture,
And a painting tells a tale,
The poet spills an image in ink,
The sculptor forms in Braille.

Not all art is touchable,
But every form is felt,
By every fibre we muster up,
Absorbed within ourselves.

Dominic Prempeh

Soothing Songs Of Old

Who is singing that song?
Nyarko!
No wonder, melody runs through her veins!

And, that song…!
That cajoles the gods to sleep with us
Under the leaky thatch of our fore-builders
And make them bow to the dictates of a common flesh;
That song invites the angels
And mesmerizes them not to go back again,
But wish they become mere mortals;
That song that attracts the wicked to us,
Not for sinister but to share love.
That song!

Just hum that song, Nyarko,
And the world shall be at peace;
Sing to the ordinary human
And all shall be well.

Marianne Larsen Reninger

Circumstances of Creation

The painter inspires the poet, the poet reflects the soul of the art.

The blank, white canvass, in its terrible absence, challenges as

"Thou, silent form, doest tease us out of thought."

Keats, inhabits his Grecian Urn, its frolic to impart.

Rilke pens his "Torso of Apollo" with rapid pulse and pounding heart.

Words create Images; Images create Words.

Chicken or the Egg/ Egg or Chicken, or any combination of the two.

A conversation. A collaboration. An omelette...

The painting, a challenge, to become part of the creation

Of an elaborate comment on life's meditation.

Ekphrasis, words describing art as writing between, in, and through

With prose, script, and letters, forms in their own right.

The blank, white canvass begins to sing and speak

With verbal texture, and rainbow hues, an expression of visual art.

All because the artist didn't know, he'd put the horse before the cart.

Author's note:
"Thou, silent form, doest tease us out of thought.": John Keats, 'Ode to a Grecian Urn'

Ekphrasis (Ἔκφρασις): verbal description of a visual work of art. An "ekphrastic poem" is a poem inspired or stimulated by a work of art. [Wikipedia]

Kirti Sharma

Lines and Tunes

It's magical, how one pens down the feelings,
in colors and emotions and many sheets.
A pinch of the glitter which still remains,
is added by a soul that converts it into music.
Cleared throats and a melodious voice,
all the emotions in this rhythmic vibe.
The joy comes in singing each line,
the smile comes as they dance between the lines.
The celebrations are made through the beats,
the girl swirls and swings along the tune.
What else do the artists need,
than the crowd living in their art?
It's a miracle, that
how for one person it's poetry
and for another it's a song.
Just the conversion of art forms.

Pamela Sinicrope

Musicians Pass the Art of Precise Execution that Springs Wings

After Ellen Dinwiddie Smith, Hornist, Minnesota Orchestra,
and my son, Anthony

Musicians execute like chemists, elements

measured to render art from talent—I watch.

Marilyn-colored hair drops a carpet square, releases

spit as she smiles—speaks revealing Texas roots.

He plays for her and I rewind eight years to the day

he held his first shiny horn, like fool's gold.

He blew into the mouthpiece to elicit—nothing,

then graduated to the call of a dying goose.

He grew into his horn: now it fits

like a pair of favorite jeans. My heart sinks

then rises with each note, inspired

by his improvement, by his teachers.

She sits upright like the back of a stiff chair,

bowing wind with breath, translating song behind

a hand-blossomed bell that billows

like morning fog in a mountaintop field—a richness

melding brass to woodwind to string that transposes
audition to gustation—churned butter or a perfect pinot noir.
Side by side, she watches as he plays,
uses figurative language and mirrors

with the skill of a poet to shape
an embouchure, lighten fingers, pitch a note—
help him unlock his soul, lift sounds
that slip wings on the listener's back.

Udaya R. Tennakoon

Poet a Weaver Bird

A poet is a weaver bird who gathers life experience
Through the mirror of wisdom uses eye lens relevance
Conceived seeds in mind give pain for a birth of diligence
Until the dream may come true struggles in a sentence

Tiny baby grows up crying, laughing and prattling
Poet feeds milk of art with the beauty of embracing
Art of language derives from words of imaging
Weaver´s home built patiently paints it shaping

Without a vision, art and beauty to the universe
Inside darkness may remain without a candle love
Poet brings a firefly into the poem to eliminate dim
Sake of art and sake of beings it may light the soul and heart

Tze-Min Ition Tsai

Barbarian Beauties

Brilliant Color clothing, RUBIK stealth in the group of beauties

Rotation layers, aligned grids, leisurely dance

The small square, Miss POCKET

Twisting her waist, petite but indulge in emotions

The dance of the box,

always like to earn people's exclamations again and again

PROFESSOR's and V-FAMILY's sisters rush on like a swarm of
hornets

comes in a continuous stream, vie with others for glamor

Who should I lose my heart to?

In this festival, who is the Queen?

Mature charm, plump the body and prettily are all can't keep anything to
itself

Increased one more surface, PENTAGON

Magic belong to PYRAMIN

Sliding that snake-like skin, MASTERMORPHIX

Crossing the ridge, FISHER

All with obscure axioms waiting to be conquered

How wonderful my concubines

How beautiful these cubes are

Dance the breath of life in the spring

In that kneading, feeding that playfulness has to touchdown

Preoccupied In my Rubik's Cubes

Author's note:

Rubik's Cubes, in my feelings, like the combination of mathematics and magic, are an incredibly beautiful art, long-term comfort my heart, when I need to calm down.

RUBIK, Miss POCKET, PROFESSOR, V-FAMILY, PENTAGON, PYRAMIN, MASTERMORPHIX and FISHER, as mentioned in this poem, are names of special shapes of the Rubik's Cubes.

Savita Tyagi

An Ode To A Doll Maker

Once I saw a little girl playing with a dancer doll.

Her outfit was embroidered with the silk and silver yarn,

And decorated carefully with gold beads and sequins.

Her scarf was as wavy and transparent as a clear mountain stream.

Colorful tinsels were braided in her black hair.

Her bow like brow and nectar dripping lips,

Her slender waist and round sensuous breast,

Were perhaps an accomplice to its maker's own sensuality.

O! Doll maker! amazing is your skill to replicate

The curves and contours of Nature's stunning creations.

The artistic hands of yours take the raw material and

Set it into the exquisite pieces of your imagination.

An angel in stone seems to fly at your command.

A figurine in porcelain sings the high notes of music.

A Kathakalli dancer comes alive in swirling motions.

The spirit of Kachina doll has the essence of spiritual force.

A silent history of Universe is depicted in these still forms.

Like a writer's verse your doll is just one of a kind.

Like a poet and his poem, you and your doll are

Solace to each other, united in a single expression of love.

The maker of the doll and the little girl playing with it,

The poet with its poetry and the mesmerized readers–

All are bound to each other with a creative rhythm

Beating in their hearts, surging in the play of ever changing

Everlasting and ever new beauty of art.

Author's note:
Kathakalli is an ancient and popular dance form of India.

Hans Van Rostenberghe

Oh Poet, Oh Poetry

Oh poet, Oh poem, Oh poetry,

It is you who will change the world

From a wall infested street

To a magnificent orchard

To an adorable lavender field

Is it not you helping the world?

To see the magic in a drop of dew

Words rolling like breaking waves

To see the wonder in the monsoon

To see the miracles in normal days

It is you moving, softening hearts

To forgive, to create peace

To fill this world with loving minds

To dream the heavenliest dream

To make us kind and kind and kind

Is it not you, dear poetry,

Who will unchain us from avarice
And destroy disabling greed
Who will spray a soft and gentle mist
Of all-encompassing unconditional love

Poetry, hope for the future
Mover of souls
Mover of minds
Mover of hearts
Hope for the world

Mithilesh Kumar Yadav

Bharatanatyam

The great Indian dance

Nature's best beauty to dress
From love to death, life to express
Devotion, creation, happiness
Sadness to war, in all its forms

Eyes with meanings, lips with words
Millions expressed, not a single spoken
Cheeks also express as the eyebrows define
Face replicates the best of divine

Hands in swing to curve the sky
Wings of music to let emotions fly
Some time just on flutes
Several times the beats of drums are high

Ghungroos tinkling around the ankles
More louder and faster than hearts can beat
Love is narrated, spirituality, war or fairy tales

Nature is expressed may it be rain, cold waves or heat

Thundering body speaking without words
Every move and step preaching a great culture to world
The culture of love, peace and humanity
The dance of God on Lands of God in its divinity

at nightfall
the whistling of the wind —
a Plainchant

Fabrizio Frosini, Haiku

ABOUT THE AUTHORS

Alexandro Acevedo Johns, Chile

— My name is Alexandro Acevedo Johns, but I sign my writing with my maternal surname (Johns). I am Chilean, born on November 2, 1947. I'm a lawyer and live in Santiago, the capital of Chile, with my wife Marcela. In my youth I was devoted to poetry, as many of my generation. Now, since I retired from the legal profession, I've regained my freedom to write. It is said that writing is a very demanding activity and endanger the spirit if you're not an optimist. But, after the years, I feel that writing helps me to stay alive and connected emotionally with the world we live in.

~*~

Ellias Aghili Dehnavi, Iran

— Born in Iran in 1996, I'm currently living with my family in Esfahan, the cultural capital of my country. I'm studying English literature at the University of Esfahan (B.A student). My favorite fields of study are poetry and English literature. I wrote my first poem, a limerick, when I was twelve years old, and compiled my first Poetry collection, with peace as a topic, when I was 15. One year later, this poetry collection got a recognition from the faculty of foreign languages (University of Isfahan/Esfahan), and also hit an important festival in Iran, called "Khawrazmi". Since then, I've published some other poetry books, also with friends, members of the M.O.P. (Messengers of Peace) international group of which I'm currently the second secretary. Since we are all seeking for a better world, where peace and friendships are basic values, it's a honor to be part of 'Poets Unite Worldwide'.

~*~

Saadat Tahir Ali, Pakistan (currently in Saudi Arabia)

— I was born (in Jan. 1965) and bred in Pakistan. A medical doctor by profession, with postgraduate qualifications in Radiology, I'm currently living in Qaseem, Saudi Arabia. My hobbies include indoor plants, interiors and woodwork.. and making friends. Over the years, I have traveled to many countries and as a reasonably experienced traveler, I am a senior reviewer on travel and foodie sites. I like nature landscapes architecture and history. I am averse to concrete jungles. I am a diehard audiophile. I consider myself a wide eyed student, ready to listen, learn and improve. I loved poetry when I was at school, started writing decades back while at cadet high continued through to King Edward Medical College. Freedom from bondage in all forms and colours, love and universal brotherhood are my cherished values. I am an incorrigible romanticist and love music. I write my mind..

~*~

Anna Banasiak, Poland

— Born in Poland in 1984, I live in Łódź, in the central part of the Country. I'm a poet and literary critic. The winner of poetry competitions in London, Berlin and Bratislava, my poetry can be found in most of the Anthologies published by F. Frosini & Poets Unite Worldwide. I'm interested in Art and psychology.

~*~

Lawrence Beck, USA

— Born in 1953, I live in Elkhorn, Nebraska, with my wife and two of my four children. My wife and I are not native to this blandly attractive, relentlessly sunny area. We grew up in the Pacific Northwest, which features spectacular scenery, but also quite gloomy weather. I have brought that gloom with me, and it often shows up in my poems. Though I graduated from college, my degrees are in economics, not English or literature. I currently work part-time hauling freight in the back of a department store. My background, my distance from the "lit-crit" department/workshop hothouse, and my real-world job probably help to give my poems their unusual matter-of-factness. So, too, does my intense admiration for Elizabethan English poetry. I honestly believe that English language poetry, for the most part, steadily has declined since that era.

~*~

Tatiana Berdennikova (*Tati Ninaria*), Russia/The Netherlands

— Tati Ninaria is my pen name, which sounds more poetic and is easier to pronounce in comparison to my real name, Tatiana Berdennikova. I was born in Moscow [then, USSR], in 1960 at the peak of the Cold War. Being a daughter of a diplomat I had a rare opportunity to travel the world from an early age. I started my carrier at different diplomatic institutions of the USSR in the United States and later worked at several international organizations. I graduated from the Moscow State Linguistic University but I never worked as a professional linguist, dedicating myself to my family's needs. Poetry is more of a hobby to me, a desire for self-realization, which gives me tremendous spiritual satisfaction. My other hobbies include reading, music, yoga and Alpine skiing. I currently live in The Hague, Netherlands.

~*~

Tom Billsborough, UK

— I was born in 1943 in Preston, England, and currently live in Kirkham, North Lancashire. I'm a retired chartered Accountant. I write poetry in English & French, and translate from French & Spanish.

~*~

Judith Blatherwick, UK

— Born 12 October 1964, I am English, but have lived in East Lothian, Scotland since 2001.

~*~

Daniel Brick, USA

— I was born in Minnesota, in the Twin Cities, in 1947 and lived my whole life here. This is where I am rooted, near the Mississippi River, in a landscape of four seasons with many trees and parks and lakes. These are the natural things I treasure. Poetry and classical music are my passions. Over the years most of my friends have moved to warmer climates, so in old age I find myself to be something of a loner. But I have a talent for solitude. A good number of my poems are published in the ebook "The Double Door".

~*~

Réne Curtis, South Africa

— Born 1975, I reside in Cape Town, the southernmost tip of Africa. I am a wife, a mother to two awesome boys. I am blessed to be a stay at home mom although I do contractual work as a graphic designer. I have fallen in love with poetry, we all need a place to be true to ourselves and I have found it in poems.

~*~

Sheryl Deane, South Africa (currently in UAE)

— I was born in 1963 in Cape Town, South Africa, but currently living in Abu Dhabi, UAE. A musician and Concert Organizer by profession, I write in my spare time. I completed my studies in English and Music at the University of Natal, KZN, South Africa, where I obtained a B.Mus (Hons). My father and mother read me many poems as a child, including poems by Wordsworth, Blake, Keats, Yeats and TS Eliot: it became a way of thinking from an early age. I started to write after my father died. My poetry is inspired by modern poets like Ted Hughes, Olive Schreiner and Bessie Head. Writers such as Roald Dahl, C.S. Lewis, Terry Pratchet are a favourite inspiration. My short story, "Time to Jump", won first Prize in a Whisper Poetry 2016 edition.

~*~

Asavri Dhillon, India (currently in Canada)

— I was born the 18th of June 1998 in Chandigarh, India. I finished high school (with medical subjects) in Chandigarh in May 2016; then, to pursue higher education, in December 2016 I moved to Oshawa, Ontario, Canada, where I'm a student of General Sciences at Durham College. I love poetry: I started writing at the age of fourteen and joined 'Poets Unite Worldwide' in 2016. My poetry can be found in many of their Anthologies. I believe in 'Humanity' (it is my sole religion), and I value 'words' more than 'actions', because actions can kill, words can't. I wish the world was united and not divided. I blog at thetravelofsteppingstones.wordpress.com, where I write about my personal experiences, views and life. In my free time I write, sketch and do photography.

~*~

Karen Edwards, USA

— I am an American poet who lives in Springtown, Texas. I was born in the state of Ohio in 1967. I am a mother, grandmother and survivor of domestic violence, with a passion for writing poetry. My first poetry chapbook, "Tears of the Soul", a collection of poems about domestic violence, was published in 1995. I have also had poems published in other anthologies and have self-published two books.

~*~

Kemurl Fofanah, Sierra Leone

— Born on the 19th of June 1992, my full name is Mustapha Abdul Kemurl Fofanah and I'm a Sierra Leonean Poet, freelance writer and a child & human rights activist. I'm currently residing in Freetown, the capital of Sierra Leone, where I'm pursuing my career in poetry and doing my degree in peace and conflicts studies at the University of Sierra Leone, Fourah Bay College —where I'm one of the only two current student Poet laureate of the English Department. A number of my poems have been published in anthologies, including a few with "Poets Unite Worldwide".

~*~

Fabrizio Frosini, Italy

— Born in Tuscany in 1953. Currently living close to Florence and to Vinci, Leonardo's hometown. Doctor in Medicine, specialized in Neurosurgery, with an ancient passion for Poetry. Author of over 2,000 poems, in 16 collections. Thirteen of them are also published as ebooks —among them: «The Chinese Gardens», «Prelude to the Night», and «Karumi – Haiku & Tanka» Author's Page at Amazon: *https://www.amazon.com/Fabrizio-Frosini/e/B014HA8ZUA/*

~*~

Alem Hailu G/Kristos, Ethiopia

— Since in Ethiopia we use our age-old style to name a new born child (chosen Name, Father's Name, Grandfather's Name): Alem is my name, Hailu is my father's name and G/Kristos is my grandfather's name. Born in Ethiopia in 1974, I live in Addis Ababa, Ethiopia capital city, where I'm currently deputy Editor-in-Chief of the Ethiopian Herald. M.A holder in literature, from Addis Ababa University, I'm a published poet, novelist, editor, translator of masterpieces, literary critic, playwright and journalist. My book "Pupils' Poems" has been published by Lulu (ISBN 978-1-329-

30770-4), and my novel "Hope from the Debris of Hopelessness" by Noah Books (2017, ISBN-10: 194811707X).

~*~

Negar Gorji, Iran

— Born in 1995, I'm an Iranian girl from Isfahan (in ancient time it was the capital of Persia: after a Persian proverb, "Esfahān nesf-e- jahān ast" – Isfahan is half of the world). I'm an M.A. student of English Literature at Alzahra University, and love writing poetry and short novels –my favorite is to write about how I see the world, and I'll tell you that I'm really looking for Peace. A few years ago, two of my short stories were published in "Etela'ate Haftegi" magazine. Poems of mine are in several Anthologies published by F. Frosini & Poets Unite Worldwide.

~*~

Simone Inez Harriman, New Zealand

— New Zealand is my native country. I was born in Christchurch, in the South Island, in 1959, and I now reside in the heart of Northland (in Māori: Te Tai Tokerau; it is the northernmost region in North Island). I live with my husband in a serene valley with her mountain, her trees, her streams and green fields, that capture, heal, calm and enchant me. I have a very rich, demanding and rewarding career in nursing. So in between shift work I spend as much spare time as I can on poetry for rest and relaxation. I am a quiet reflective person. I enjoy gardening, reading, and motorcycle riding.

~*~

Birgitta Abimbola Heikka, Nigeria/USA

— I was born in Lagos, Nigeria, in 1960 (the year of "equality" for many African countries), to a Swedish father and a Nigerian mother. I moved to the U.S. in 1987. I'm currently living in the state of Maryland. I have two wonderful daughters.

~*~

Afrooz Jafarinoor, Iran

— I'm a teacher and writer, living in Tehran. I was born in 1972 in

Hamedan, Iran, from lower middle class parents who loved books and raised me with lots of fairy tales. Learning Persian, Turkish, and Kurdish as a child has given me a passion for foreign languages. I hold a master's degree in English literature, and have also learned a lot of German. I write poetry in Persian and English and also translate into them. Another field I love is theater and cinema. I also hold a master's degree in dramatic literature and I write reviews. To publish my poetical compositions and translations, as well as my critical essays, I launched a website: *www.poetsrepublic.com.*

~*~

Seema Jayaraman, India

— I was born in 1972 in Kannur (Cannanore), Kerala – God's own country – and now live in Mumbai. I did my post-graduation in Science with a few additional degrees in Management to assist my job functions. I juggle multiple roles, a full time working Mom of two little boys, working in Information Technology domain for a multinational Bank. Constantly struggling to balance various demands, I find myself trying to record the creative thoughts constantly churning in my mind. As an Airforce child, I have travelled extensively within India, absorbing India's myriad hues and cultures. Thanks to my IT career, I gained exposures to varied international cultures, mainly in USA, experiencing the splendor of their vast countryside and snowcapped mountains. My roots are from the ancient land of 'Naura' or Malabar, now known as Kannur, the land of lores and looms. The seeds for Poetry were sown in early childhood, with practice of reciting Hindu shlokas supervised by elders, later by encouragements of my school teachers. My first poem, as a 12 year old, got published in my school magazine. However, eventually life caught up and my writings became sporadic. In September 2015, the images of a little boy washed up ashore the Aegean sea, a victim of the ongoing Syrian refugee crisis, brought the world to its knees. In anguish, I found myself penning verses —I was writing after a hiatus of 20 years.

~*~

Srijana KC Rayamajhi, Nepal

— I was born in 1990, in Kathmandu. I have two siblings. My father being in Nepal army, I went to the army school. I am a doctor by profession. I write both to express myself and for my love for Art and Creativity. Besides, I like painting, reading books, visiting places, trekking at times. Yet, sleeping is what I'd like the most, if only I could... I try to listen to Buddha's words and therefore pursue peace since childhood. My name, Srijana, in Nepali means 'Creation'. My poems are 'born of heart', Manasija. My poems are 'born of mind', Manoj.

~*~

Joji Varghese Kuncheria, India (currently in Oman)

— I'm an Indian national working in Muscat, Oman, since 2004. I was born on February 14, 1953, in India. I did my M.A. in English literature from Christ Church College, Kanpur (Kanpur University, India). I'm a senior Lecturer, teaching British and American literature to the undergraduate students in a college in Oman. I started writing poems while I was working as a teacher in Ethiopia (1978–1985) and have continued to write, after a long gap, from 2009 onwards. I'm very passionate about the peaceful co-existence of the people anywhere in this planet, and cherish to see such a world order. I'm a good chess player too.

~*~

Kelly Kurt, USA

— Born 1958, I don't refer to myself as a poet or anything else other than a father of six children. During my life I've explored many avocations. I've been a competitive athlete, singer, gardener, woodworker, ravenous reader, experimenter and philosopher. I'll beam and prattle on when asked about my personal high energy accelerator lab, my time as a bodybuilder, my green thumb, days in my band or the buildings I helped to restore, but get the most joy from talking about my children. Divorced for many years, I now live in Polo (Illinois), in a 160 year old church building that I helped friends restore nearly a decade ago. In my early teens, my mother instilled a love of writing in me. Unfortunately, in my senior year of high school, my beloved mother died. But I continued to write and my words often portrayed the unfairness and pain of life. But the wonder of nature, the beauty of friendship and mystery of life in general, would alter my poetic direction. Some universal themes would still work their way into my writing, but the day to day, seemingly mundane aspects of existence began to be explored as in depth topics. I've published a book: 'Good Night, Sleep Tight: Dos & Don'ts for Bedbugs'

~*~

Eldar Kurtovic, Bosnia & Herzegovina

— I am Bosnian-American. Born in 1997 in Sarajevo, I moved to America when I was 7 years old and got back to Sarajevo at 17.

~*~

Natchai Leenders, The Netherlands

— I was born in Nijmegen, The Netherlands, in 1987, where I'm currently living. I have a Master's Degree in American Studies, specializing in literature and culture. My path of poetry started in 2007 and I've improved my craft thanks to a Creative Writing Workshop I attended from 2008 till 2011. I've performed at several open-mics from 2009 to 2013 and picked this up again this year (2016), writing under the pen name 'Riordan' (*Irish for 'King of the Bards / Bard of the Kings'*). Since September 2015, I've been trying to organize my own poetry course to inspire kids, the youth and everyone else.

~*~

Kenneth Maswabi, Botswana

— I am a Motswana born on 14th November 1977 in Maun, Botswana. A Motswana means a native of Botswana. I am currently living in Francistown, the second largest city in my country. I studied Medicine and Surgery at the University of Melbourne, Australia. Poetry to me is a journey of discovery and a way of communication (to myself and others) beyond the normal physical reality/connections. Poetry nourishes the senses, grooming them to perceive even the slightest physical/emotional/spiritual imbalances in environment or self. I look for the truth in the remotest avenues of imagination, I seek for peace and love in all areas of my life. I am for humanity & God. I believe in Genesis 1:27 "*So God created mankind in his own image, in the image of God he created them; male and female he created them.*"

~*~

Mallika Menon, India

— Born on the 23rd of January 1961, in India, I hail from Kerala's capital city, Trivandrum, on India's southern tip, but I enjoyed my life in Mumbai. Lover of music and literature, I sing songs and poems. One day, I started singing my own poems! I offer collection of poems in mother tongue

Malayalam as well as English. Simple emotions, gentle feelings and shades of empathy reflect in my poetry. I like reading philosophy. I enjoy interior decoration. I'm travel-savvy, keen to explore cultures and cuisines world-over.

~*~

Barry Middleton, USA

— I'm an American poet who has been writing for about fifty years. I was born in 1946 in a small town in Mississippi. I'm a retired mental health counselor, currently living in Sarasota, Florida.

~*~

Leloudia Migdali, Greece

— My name is Leloudia Migdali. I was born in 1959 in Itea, a nice little city close to Delphi, 'the center of world'. Attended school there till 1979, then followed a course in the English Literature Department of Aristotle University of Thessaloniki, Greece. Back to Itea, where I still live, ran my own English institute till I was appointed at the public sector. I have been teaching English for the past 29 years, in Primary, Secondary and High school as well as in the Maritime College in Galaxidi city. Meanwhile I got a postgraduate degree on Teaching English as a Foreign Language from Patras University. Happily married and mother of two children, poetry and writing have always been my favorite hobbies. After my retirement from public sector, I have been devoting more time in writing poetry.

~*~

Istvan Dan Molnar Uriel, Hungary/Sweden

— I live in Nykroppa, Varmland, Sweden, but I was born in Hungary in 1950, in a small community close to Budapest, called Fot, where I grew up. Time and expectation was always greater than what a simple life could offer: my dreams always went to the sky.. I've seen lot of falling stars all my life, even in my dreams. My life changed after military services; got married, moved to Budapest, began to study at the technical college. Before last year's ending, moved to Sweden with my wife.. A new life again, studying Swedish, even French, later English, and more languages.. I began reading a lot of books, most of them in Swedish and English. I've always liked Science, but Psychology and Philosophy were my passion: Einstein,

Sigmund Freud, Maimonides, Friedrich Hegel... After 3 children my wife wanted a divorce.. A new life again, but the details were more painful. I went to Paris for a short time. I've been a legionary, but found no consolation. Back to Sweden, I was later asked to move to Israel.. Another language to learn, again. After 13 years there I got enough, so I came back to Sweden as a retired man. Now I live in solitude, with my dreams.. mostly reading and writing poetry. Sometimes I dream about words: I like seeing words in pictures and I've begun to find connections between words and pictures... I'm currently in Ashdod, Israel.

~*~

Anitah Muwanguzi, Uganda

— I was born on December 31st 1992 in Jinja, Uganda, and I am currently living in Kampala, the capital, where I am a journalist and News Anchor at a local radio station. A fiction writer and poet, I love to paint pictures with words. I love reading, writing, clever talking and I hate to give up on anything worthwhile. I'm currently working on a couple of short stories, and pursuing a bachelor's degree in development studies at Makerere University, Kampala.

~*~

Bharati Nayak, India

— I hail from Odisha, an eastern state of India which has a great heritage of art and architecture. I was born on the 26th May 1962 and live in Bhubaneswar, capital city of Odisha. I have a Masters Degree in Political Science from Utkal University, Vani Vihar, Bhubaneswar, and have a Government job. As a bilingual writer (Odia and English), my published works include a devotional poetry anthology in Odia, 'Padma Pada', and a collection of poetry in English, 'Words Are Such Perfect Traitors'. My poems have been published in many newspapers, magazines, journals, e-books and poetry anthologies of national and international repute, such as 'Rock Pebbles', Odisha Review, Utkal Prasanga, Creation and Criticism, Literary Herald, Glimpses, 'Splash of Verse' and the like. Poems of mine are also in many Anthologies published by Fabrizio Frosini & Poets Unite Worldwide. I have a blog, 'Bharatispen', at Wordpress. I also take interest in social issues.

~*~

Valsa George Nedumthallil, India

— Born in 1953, I live in a suburb of Ernakulam, Kerala (in the south-west of India), where I lead a happy and contented life. Poetry is a late boon into my life. Only after my retirement as a teacher from a college in Kerala, India, I started writing poems. Now it has become a pleasant obsession and a rewarding engagement for me. I write on a wide spectrum of topics spanning Nature, Love and Human relations. I have to my credit four published volumes of poems: 'Beats', 'Drop of a Feather', 'Entwining Shadows' and 'Rainbow Hues', the latter two available at Amazon. I spend my time reading and writing poems. I feel that by writing poems, one can establish soul connections with the right kind of people. Love of Nature is deeply ingrained into my psyche and it is my greatest inspiration!

~*~

Mohammed Asim Nehal, India

— Born in 1970 and brought up in Nagpur, the orange city of India, I started writing poems and stories at very young age, as I was inclined to write something to express what I feel and it comes from the deep thickets of my heart. I feel poetry is a trick of language that magnetizes the readers and takes them to a world that is virtually created by the poets. A number of my poems have been published on magazines and newspapers. By profession, I am a Chartered Accountant and a Company Secretary with Master's degree in Commerce and Bachelor's degree in Law. What I studied for and what I feel are two parallel lines.

~*~

Dismas Okombo, Kenya

— Born 26th Dec.1998, I'm a Kenyan poet, from Nairobi. I've an innate passion for poetry and literature in general. Some of my poems belong in Anthologies published by Fabrizio Frosini; others are featured in 'Poetry Anthology', by Writer Guild Kenya, and on online magazines. I blog at poetdismas.WordPress.com. Besides poetry, I enjoy listening to country music and going on nature walk.

~*~

Rekha Padinjattakathu, India/Germany

— Born in 1977 in India, I am a voracious reader and an avid traveler. Passionate about nature and wildlife, I love spending time out in the wilderness. I hold a Master's degree in Computer Applications and worked several years in a multinational information technology company. I am currently pursuing a second Master's degree in Germany, where I reside with my husband and two little boys. I have a keen interest in photography and absolutely, completely and totally love writing. My work has been published and is forthcoming in several magazines. I blog in English and Malayalam, at *wherethemindisforeverfree.wordpress.com*.

~*~

Marcondes Pereira Da Silva De Mesquita, Brazil

— Born in 1991, I live in Barueri (State of São Paulo, Brazil). I'm a poet who is searching for my own truth, in this liquid world. I write to understand myself and the chaotic universe we're living in. My poetry speaks about war, love, religion, Philosophy, History and several other themes, although I write chronicles, tales and theatre plays too. My biggest influences in terms of poetry are: Camões, Petrarch, Boccaccio and Homer. I study their texts to create my own epopees, which I would like to see transformed in music. I am a technologist in Human Resources (Faculty Fernão Dias).

~*~

Sarah Louise Persson, UK

— I was born in 1966 in England, in a small town called Wellington (Telford, Shropshire). I have lived in both South Africa and Denmark but am currently living in Leeds, West Yorkshire, England.

~*~

Dominic Prempeh, Ghana

— Born in Mampong, Ashanti region of Ghana, in 1985, I hold a B.A. in Political Science with Geography and Resource Development from the University of Ghana, Legon. I am currently a High School tutor, teaching Government and Social Studies at Ofoase Senior High/Technical School in the Ashanti Region. A passionate student of Nature, I believe in equal opportunities for everyone and I love to join in any "Freedom Fight" that makes the World a "safer place to live in". Some of my poems are published in Anthologies edited by Fabrizio Frosini and Poets Unite Worldwide.

~*~

Marianne Larsen Reninger, USA

— I was born in Denmark in 1944 and emigrated to the United States with my parents in 1947. I began painting and writing at a very young age and by 16 was studying painting and taking commissions. My prime influence was a Russian born artist, Tatiana McKinney, world famous with work in the Vatican and in major museums. From Tatiana I learned to see "the atmosphere between the mountains" and the "meaning between the words". Today, I paint and write from my mountaintop home near Asheville, N.C.. I consider myself an "editorial artist" with my acrylic/collages often containing original poetry. My work is textural, touchable glimpses of the natural world and my reaction to life's political and social merry-go-round, words become as important as the brush strokes. The work is meant to be read, like a favorite book or poem, as well as, absorbed, like a visual feast. You can see my work at Pinterest.com, Marianne Reninger, Marianne's Art Board.

~*~

Kirti Sharma, India

— Born on 7th October 1996, I live in Delhi, and have completed my graduation in Life Sciences from Delhi University. I started writing poems when I was 15 years old, as that part of my life was a turning point. I realized the true happiness lies within one self. The world of poetry became a part of my life and I started reading & writing more of them. I learned how each line of a poem has its own music. The poems written by P.B. Shelly are my favorite; 'Goodnight' being one of them. I generally write poems on love and solitariness as these two conditions are common in every person's life. My poems consists of simple words & are easily understood. My other hobbies are singing, dancing and reading novels. Paulo Coelho is my favorite author.

~*~

Pamela Smith Sinicrope, USA

— I was born in Frederick, Maryland in 1970. I spent most of my youth in

Texas; and now, for the past 13 years, I have lived in Rochester, MN with my husband and three children. I have a doctorate in Public Health, with an interest in reducing morbidity and mortality from cancer through focus on families, lifestyles, and genetics. As a young child and raised as a Unitarian, I have fond memories of hiking in the woods and reading poetry while sitting on rocks and communing with nature. When I was twelve, my grandmother and I used to write letters and share our poetry with each other. I enjoy: tennis, music of all kinds, reading (poetry and prose), and spending time with my family. I returned to writing poetry over the past year in my 40's. Now that my children and I are older, I have time again, to reflect, write, and read. And I love doing it most every day!

~*~

Udaya R. Tennakoon, Sri Lanka (living in Switzerland)

— My full name is Udaya Rathna Tennakoon Mudiyanselage. As a Diaspora Poet, I live in Zürich, Switzerland, but my home country is Sri Lanka, where I was born in 1970. Being a political refugee, I could see the world in many perspectives and engage with writing and research. I graduated from University of Colombo and University of Kelaniya, Sri Lanka. At the University of Basel, Switzerland, and also at the University of Innsbruck, Austria, I studied 'Peace and Conflict Transformation' for my master Studies. As a writer, I've written some theater works and contribute articles to many websites and also as a social activist, I engage with many voluntary works inside Switzerland and Europe as well as Nepal and Sri Lanka. I've published a haiku poetry book titled 'The Fragrance of Loss' (2017).

~*~

Tze Min **Ition Tsai**, Taiwan

— My name is Ition Tsai 蔡宜勳, where 蔡 (Tsai) is my Family name, while Tze-Min Tsai 蔡澤民 is my pen name. Born in 1957 in Taiwan (Republic of China), I live in Changhua city. I hold a Ph.D. in Chemical Engineering, and a Master of Science in Applied Mathematics. I have equal affection in science, mathematics and literature; the results are all reflected in my academic and creative writings. I am an Associate Professor for Asia University, Taiwan; at the same time I am a columnist for several poetry journals as well as the editor of "Reading, Writing and Teaching" academic text for the National Changhua Normal University, Taiwan. My writing includes novels, prose, and poetry, and I specialize in describing nature and humanity's love and affection through these creative literary works (for such a reason I am often referred to as a "green poet"). In addition to receiving many domestic and foreign literary awards, a large number of my works have been translated into more than 13 languages in over 37 countries.

~*~

Savita Tyagi, India/USA

— Born in 1948, I was raised in India. As a student of liberal arts I loved history and literature and completed my M.A. in Western History. After marriage I migrated to California and later came to live in Edmond, Oklahoma, where I reside currently with my husband of 46 years. In U.S. for some time my love for reading was limited to English language. However the need to expose our children to their language, culture and religion brought me back to my roots. While organizing children's classes at my home and temple, I started studying more of our spiritual books, in English as well as in Sanskrit, and realized that some of the best poetry was hidden in the ancient literature. While ancient poetry takes me to the path of self discovery, the contemporary writings help strengthen the social consciousness. Some of my poems have been published in newspapers, anthologies and magazines. A self published book of poems 'Back Yard Poetry' is available through Blurb. But most of my poetry and other writings are on my blog 'When Thoughts Get Wings'. Besides reading and writing I enjoy walking, quilting, meditating, learning from Nature and visiting with friends. I am moderate in my views and have deep respect for human values that nurture and nourish us in all walks of life.

~*~

Hans Van Rostenberghe, Belgium/Malaysia

— Born on October 18th 1964, in Oudenaarde, Belgium, I'm currently living in a town called Bachok, in Kelantan State, Malaysia. I am a doctor in medicine (neonatologist) and a professor at Universiti Sains Malaysia, where I have been working since 1994. Among the most important sources of inspiration in my life are Dr. Albert Schweitzer, Dr. Martin Luther King and the Organization 'Médécins sans Frontieres'. Poetry has become a passion since 2010, when I was bedridden for three months, due to a fractured vertebra: I write under the pseudonym 'Aufie Zophy'. I am a reader of philosophy, a nature lover and a family man. I believe strongly that the world is heading towards harmony through an ever increasing kindness revolution which is close to its sharp inflection point on its exponential curve. My blog: *http://reflectionsbyhans.blogspot.com/*

~*~

Mithilesh Kumar Yadav, India

— I was born on 14th September 1985 (on our National Language Day), in holy city of Gorakhpur, a district in Uttar Pradesh, India, where I live. Since I believe that the biggest service to mankind is to awake oneself and get to self-actualization, I chose the pen-name 'Soum' (one of the names of 'Sun' in Indian mythology; as an example of detachment, dedication, truth, awakening and love). I did Bachelors of Pharmacy (B. Pharmacy) from H.I.M.T. College of Pharmacy, Greater Noida, in 2009, and I'm a pharmacist by profession. I love writing poems and painting.

~*~

Poets Unite Worldwide

'Poets Unite Worldwide' represents, in my mind, an invitation and an appeal (*"Poets worldwide, unite!"*), and it is more an open group of poets, an independent community, than a formal association —but still an 'Association' of over two hundred free minds and spirits.

I'd say that this comes, first, from my own nature: I consider myself not just an Italian, but a Citizen of the World —born in Italy by chance—, equal to everybody else: all human beings on planet Earth, in brotherhood. I have an independent mind and the utmost respect for the human values of freedom, justice, privacy.. and I dislike almost all kind of formalities: for such reason I stay away from anything that sounds bureaucratic.

Although living in different countries and continents, we all feel a kinship, being part of this poetic drive for worldwide peace and brotherhood. In such a way, we work together for the highest purposes, as all mankind should do.

I can say that 'Poets Unite Worldwide' was born, in its extended form, in the Autumn of 2015, when I invited tens and tens of poets, worldwide, to join me in writing a poetry compilation on (against) terror, in response to the bloody Paris events of November 13, 2015.

I felt the urge, that time, to began working on a new ebook, 'Poetry Against Terror', and I enlisted 'my' community of poets worldwide to help, since I wanted it to become a large collective work: the voice of poets from many different countries, worldwide, who stand up and speak aloud, but without hatred, against the bloody madness of terror. Astonishingly, 64 Poets from 43 countries lent their pens in the effort, and I wrote, in the introductory note to the book, "we—poets of the world—wish to make our voices resonate in the minds and hearts of all women and men who refuse to be silenced by hate and violence." Pamela Sinicrope and Daniel Brick, both of Minnesota, USA, along with Richard Thézé, England, co-edited the collection of diverse poems about terrorism —in Paris and around the world. Cover art was by Galina Italyanskaya, Russia.

The project came together quickly, with poets coming from countries in all continents, including Arab/Islamic countries: *Australia, Bangladesh, Botswana, Brazil, Canada, Chile, China, Croatia, Egypt, France, Germany, Ghana, Greece, India, Indonesia, Iran, Ireland, Israel, Italy, Kenya, Morocco, New Zealand, Nepal, Nigeria, Oman, Pakistan, The Philippines, Qatar, Russia, Saudi Arabia, Serbia, Somalia, South Africa, Sri Lanka, Sweden, Switzerland, Thailand, Tunisia, United Arab Emirates, Uganda, United Kingdom, USA, Zimbabwe.*

Poem topics range from a focus on the liberty of France, to the musings of a mother who does not want her child suffering from terrorism, to a young woman who incessantly searches Google for the answers to the terrorism problem, to the story of African villagers who drink from a cow's horn under a peaceful moon until terrorism takes over. Many of the poets have experienced terrorism first-hand, and this witness is expressed in their writings and their biographies. As Pamela Sinicrope said, "We've all been touched by terrorism. For some, the topic hit home after the events in Paris, but for others, terrorism has been a disturbing part of everyday life — these facts are borne out in the poems. The poems speak for themselves."

Yet, as a group of poets collaborating together on a variety of projects, we didn't stop with that first book. We do have a website, that Udaya Tennakon created, as well as a Fb page. Since then, we've been continually publishing and growing, and –hopefully– improving as writers.

In Spring 2016 we published the ebook 'Poets Against Inequality', to add our voice to those other unequivocal voices that denounce an absolute lack of equality in our society. The poems collected in that book (as well as the previous one) belong in what is called "Poetry of Witness", and we believe that this is a task that all of us, as poets, have a moral obligation to pursue, because we can't accept to live in a world where extreme poverty is so widespread and sheer inequality is the norm.

Another project accomplished is a book on the Refugees theme: in March 2016, while looking at an image taken on the border between Greece and Macedonia, I felt the urge to write a poem. From that urge, a new editorial project was born, the book 'By Land & By Seas'; then others followed, like 'We All Are Persons – Why Gender Discrimination?', and 'Time to show up – Poetry for Democracy'. And surely, after the present book, thanking the enthusiasm and energy of many in our group, new good projects will follow. Our mission keeps on.

(Fabrizio Frosini, on behalf of 'Poets Unite Worldwide')

From the same Publisher

(*BE*: Bilingual Editions, English–Italian
Texts translated into Italian by F. Frosini)

Anthologies in Paperbacks:

– 'Fifty-six Female Voices of Contemporary Poetry' – English Ed.;
– 'From an Old Path – Contemporary European Poetry' – English Ed.;
– 'Tunes from the Indian Subcontinent – Contemporary Poetry' – English Ed.;
– 'The Sounds of America – Contemporary American Poetry' – English Ed.;
– 'Whispering to the Heart – Contemporary African Poetry' – English Ed.;
– 'Hues of the World – Contemporary Poetry' – English Ed.;
– 'Singing Together – Poems for Christmas' – English Ed.;
– 'Let's Laugh Together – Poems for Children' – English Ed.;
– 'When Love is Bitter' – English Ed.;
– 'Through Time, Through Space' – English Ed.;
– 'Homo Homini Lupus: Why To kill a Mockingbird?' – English Ed.;
– 'United We Stand – Poets Against Terror' – English Ed.;
– 'We All Are Persons – Why Gender Discrimination?' – English Ed.;
– 'Time to show up – Poetry for Democracy' – English Ed.;
– 'Our Only World – Poetry for Planet Earth' – English Ed.;
– 'A Note, A Word, A Brush – Ode To The Arts' – English Ed.;
– 'Winter Melodies' – English Edition.

Anthologies in Ebooks:

– 'At The Crossing Of Seven Winds' – English Ed.;
– 'Nine Tales Of Creation' – English Ed.;
– 'Scattering Dreams & Tales' – English Ed.;
– 'We Are The Words – Siamo Parole' – *BE*;

– 'Whispers to the World – Sussurri al Mondo" – *BE*;
– 'The Double Door' by Daniel J. Brick & Fabrizio Frosini – English Ed.;
– 'Poetry Against Terror'– English Ed.;
– 'How to write Poetry, A Handbook – Come scrivere Poesie, Manuale'– *BE*;
– 'Poets Against Inequality'– English Ed.;
– 'By Land & By Seas – Poetry for the Refugees' – English Ed.;
– 'Voices without veils' – English Ed.;
– 'Singing Together – Poems for Christmas' – English Ed.;
– 'We All Are Persons – Why Gender Discrimination?' – English Ed.;
– 'A Note, a Word, a Brush – Ode to the Arts' – English Ed.;
– 'Seasons of the Fleeting World – Writing Haiku' – English Ed.;
– 'Our Chains, Our Dreams' [Part One] – English Ed.;
– 'Our Chains, Our Dreams' [Part Two] – English Ed.;
– 'Our Chains, Our Dreams' [Part Three] – English Ed.;
– 'Our Only World – Poetry for Planet Earth' – English Ed.;
– 'Time to show up – Poetry for Democracy' – English Ed.;
– 'Let's Laugh Together – Poems for Children' – English Ed.;
– 'Moments of Lightness – Haiku & Tanka' – English Ed.;
– 'United We Stand – Poets Against Terror' – English Ed.;
– 'When Love is Bitter' – English Ed.;
– 'From an Old Path – Contemporary European Poetry' – English Ed.;
– 'Tunes from the Indian Subcontinent – Contemporary Poetry' – English Ed.;
– 'Whispering to the Heart – Contemporary African Poetry' – English Ed.;
– 'Hues of the World – Contemporary Poetry' – English Ed.;
– 'The Sounds of America – Contemporary American Poetry' – English Ed.;
– 'Fifty-six Female Voices – Poetry by Poets Unite Worldwide' – English Ed.;
- 'Homo Homini Lupus: Why To kill a Mockingbird?' – English Ed.;
- 'Essays on the World of Humans' – by D.J. Brick & F. Frosini – English Ed.;
- 'Through Time, Through Space' – English Ed.;
– 'Winter Melodies' – English Edition.

Under publication:
– 'Spring Songs' – English Edition.

Books by Fabrizio Frosini as sole Author:

– «The Chinese Gardens – English Poems» – English Ed. – (published also in Italian Ed.:
  – «I Giardini Cinesi» – Edizione Italiana);
  – «KARUMI – Haiku & Tanka» – Italian Ed.;
  – «Allo Specchio di Me Stesso» ('In the Mirror of Myself') – Italian Ed.;
  – «Il Vento e il Fiume» ('The Wind and the River') – Italian Ed.;
  – «A Chisciotte» ('To Quixote') – Italian Ed.;
  – «Il Puro, l'Impuro – Kosher/Treyf» ('The pure, the Impure – Kosher / Treyf') – Italian Ed.;
  – «Frammenti di Memoria – Carmina et Fragmenta» ('Fragments of Memories') – Italian Ed.;
  – «La Città dei Vivi e dei Morti» ('The City of the Living and the Dead') – Italian Ed.;
  – «Nella luce confusa del crepuscolo» ('In the fuzzy light of the Twilight') – Italian Ed.;
  – «La Chiave dei Sogni» ('The Key to Dreams') – Italian Ed.;
  – «Echi e Rompicapi» ('Puzzles & Echoes') – Italian Ed.;
  – «Ballate e Altre Cadenze» ('Ballads and Other Cadences') – Italian Ed.;
  – «Selected Poems – Επιλεγμένα Ποιήματα – Poesie Scelte» – Greek–English–Italian (Αγγλικά, Ελληνικά, Ιταλικά – Greek translation by Dimitrios Galanis);
  – «Prelude to the Night – English Poems» – English Edition (published also in Italian Ed.:
  – «Preludio alla Notte»).

Under publication:
  – «A Season for Everyone – Haiku & Tanka Poetry» – English Ed.
  – «Il Sentiero della Luna» ('The Moon's Path') – Italian Ed.

Where to find us

Publisher's Page:

https://www.amazon.com/Fabrizio-Frosini/e/B014HA8ZUA/

~*~

Poets Unite Worldwide:

Fb page: https://www.facebook.com/poetsuniteworldwide/

Website: https://poetsuniteworldwide.org

www.ingramcontent.com/pod-product-compliance
Lightning Source LLC
Chambersburg PA
CBHW071506220526
45472CB00003B/933